THE SIMPLE

BUTTERCREAM

FROSTING COOKBOOK

STAICEY M LEOYED

INTRODUCTION

Hello there, my fellow frosting aficionados, and welcome to "The Simple Buttercream Frosting Cookbook," your comprehensive guide to the smooth and flavorful world of buttercream icing. This is not just a cookbook but a creative adventure into the heart of baking and decoration, specifically designed for beginners and pros alike, aiming to help you perfect the delicate art of buttercream frosting.

This book is your one-stop solution to mastering buttercream - the sweet and creamy elixir that makes our cakes, cupcakes, and pastries not only look irresistible but taste divine. The magical allure of buttercream lies in its simplicity and versatility. It's a frosting chameleon, easily customizable to match the flavor profile of any dessert, with a texture that lends itself perfectly to decorating.

Imagine a universe where you have the perfect buttercream recipe at your fingertips, making every celebration more unique, every dessert more tantalizing. "The Simple Buttercream Frosting Cookbook" is your portal into that universe. We begin our journey with the "Buttercream Basics," an in-depth look at the core of buttercream, its types, its versatility, and its sheer decadence.

Next, in "Buttercream Tips," we equip you with the best advice from industry professionals and seasoned home bakers. Master the subtle art of whipping, avoid curdling, discover the perfect sugar to butter ratio, and learn how to create a light, fluffy buttercream that will melt in your mouth and enchant your taste buds.

We then delve into the diverse world of "Buttercream Ingredients," because knowing your ingredients is just as important as knowing the recipe. Uncover the secrets of the essential ingredients used in various buttercream recipes, from basic to gourmet, and the pivotal role each one plays in creating the perfect texture and flavor.

The chapters that follow are a symphony of flavors, from classic "American Buttercream" to the velvety "Swiss Meringue Buttercream," each with their unique charms. Embark on a delightful journey to explore the rich flavors of "German Buttercream," the luxurious "French Buttercream," and the smooth, sweet notes of the "Italian Meringue Buttercream."

Next, we offer you an array of inspired recipes, like the "Morning Joy Coffee Buttercream," "Quick and Simple Buttercream," "Cream Cheese Dream Buttercream," and more. Get ready to explore buttercream versions that take inspiration from different cuisines, cultures, and even festivities.

Chocolate lovers rejoice! We have a special corner dedicated to you, with recipes like "Dark Horse Chocolate Cream Cheese Buttercream," "German Chocolate Buttercream," and the dreamy "Chocolate Marshmallow Fondant." And let's not forget our cheese lovers, who will find delectable delights like "Strawberry Cream Cheese Frosting" and "Amaretto-Maple Cream Cheese Buttercream."

For the adventurous at heart, we have the intriguing "Avocado Buttercream," the sophisticated "Champagne Buttercream," and the nostalgic "Christmas Eggnog Buttercream." Then there's the "Go Nuts Cream Cheese Buttercream," a nutty surprise that will leave you craving more.

As a bonus, we've included recipes for cakes that provide the perfect canvas for your buttercream creations. "Chocolate Cake Prague," "Black Forest Meringue Chocolate Cake," "White Chocolate Raspberry Cheesecake," and "Tropical Paradise Carrot Cake," are just a few of the delicious bases you can dress up with our buttercream recipes.

"The Simple Buttercream Frosting Cookbook" is more than just a collection of recipes; it's an invitation to experiment, to learn, to taste, and above all, to enjoy. Whether you're a novice baker just starting your buttercream journey or a seasoned chef looking to expand your frosting repertoire, this book offers something for everyone.

Here's to a sweet, buttery, and flavorful journey into the land of buttercream. Welcome to "The Simple Buttercream Frosting Cookbook." Let the adventure begin!

"The Simple Buttercream Frosting Cookbook" also pays homage to fruit-inspired buttercreams. From the tropical "Banana Buttercream" and "Paradise Island Buttercream," to the tangy "Lemon Cream Cheese Buttercream" and the "Raspberry Buttercream," these recipes add a fresh, fruity dimension to our buttercream spectrum. And if you've ever wondered what the tropics taste like, the "Tropical Paradise Carrot Cake" with its luscious buttercream topping will transport you to a sunny beach with every bite.

For those who fancy something slightly different, the "Unbaked Meringue Icing" and "Marzipan Icing" provide delightful diversions from the traditional buttercream recipes.

As you navigate through this book, you'll discover that buttercream isn't just a topping; it's an expression of creativity. It can be tailored to match the occasion, the season, or even the mood. The "Silver Mountain Buttercream" is perfect for winter-themed cakes, while the "Hazelnut Buttercream" evokes the warmth of fall. If you're celebrating love, the "Champagne Buttercream" would be just the ticket.

Let's also not forget our dedicated chapter on "Caramel Dreams Buttercream," a rich and indulgent treat that brings to life the sweet, decadent notes of caramel. This heavenly buttercream is a dessert by itself but when spread over a warm cake, it transports you to an entirely new dimension of gastronomic delight.

And because we want to make sure you have all the tools necessary to create your masterpieces, we've included a selection of bonus recipes that complement our diverse range of buttercreams. Experiment with the intense "Chocolate Cake Prague," the sophisticated "Black Forest Meringue Chocolate Cake," the refreshing "White Chocolate Raspberry Cheesecake," and the exotic "Tropical Paradise Carrot Cake."

The versatility of buttercream opens the doors to endless creative possibilities. Whether you're interested in enhancing your baking skills, looking to wow your guests at the next gathering, or simply searching for the secret to perfect buttercream, "The Simple Buttercream Frosting Cookbook" has you covered.

As you delve deeper into this book, you'll realize that each page holds the potential for creating memorable moments, and each recipe is a gateway to a delightful and delicious adventure. So, get ready to set sail in this ocean of sweetness, where waves of velvety buttercream carry you towards baking excellence.

Baking, after all, isn't just about eating. It's about expressing love, celebrating life, and, most importantly, creating memories. With this book, you're not just making buttercream; you're creating joy, one delicious spoonful at a time.

We hope you find as much pleasure reading and experimenting with these recipes as we did creating them. From simple basics to innovative creations, "The Simple Buttercream Frosting Cookbook" is designed to inspire, educate, and most importantly, to satiate your sweet tooth.

Ready to stir, whisk, and frost? Let's dive into this exciting world of buttercream. Your sweet journey begins here.

CONTENTS

Buttercream Basics

There are many varieties of buttercream, but most popular kinds are American Buttercream, Swiss Meringue, Italian Meringue, and French buttercreams.

American Buttercream

American Buttercream is a combination of butter and powdered sugar in 1:2 proportion. This buttercream is a great base buttercream for adding flavors, and it is easy to make.

American Buttercream is best for decorations that require a firmer icing. It is, however, not ideal for piping flowers.

Swiss Meringue Buttercream

Swiss Meringue Buttercream is a combination of heated egg whites, sugar, and softened butter. Egg whites and sugar get whipped into a meringue. Later softened butter is added into the mixture.

Swiss Meringue Buttercream is ideal for cake exteriors, piping flowers, and icing cakes and cupcakes.

Italian Meringue Buttercream

Italian Meringue Buttercream is a combination of heated water, sugar, egg whites, and softened butter.

Italian Meringue Buttercream is ideal for cake exteriors, piping flowers, and icing cakes and cupcakes.

French Buttercream

French Buttercream is a combination of heated water and sugar. This mixture is added to egg yolks and softened butter.

French Buttercream is ideal for cake exteriors, piping flowers, and icing cakes and cupcakes.

BUTTERCREAM TIPS

Tip 1: Do not overbeat your buttercream. If you are beating butter without any additives, such as sugar, you can beat butter as long as you desire.

Butter comes in different colors: pale, yellow or orange. Typically, you will beat the butter for one to two minutes, but If you want to achieve a lighter buttercream color, beat butter for a longer time.

Tip 2: Once you added any other ingredients to the butter, limit beating to 20 to 30 seconds or less.

Tip 3: Sift powdered sugar at least one time to prevent the creation of lumps, and making a smoother buttercream.

Tip 4: When you are beating buttercream, make sure you periodically scrape the sides of the bowl and mixer blades to incorporate and evenly mix all ingredients.

Tip 5: Use cane sugar instead of beet sugar to achieve a smoother consistency.

Tip 6: If your buttercream is too stiff add water or milk, one spoon at a time.

Tip 7: If you want to use buttercream for piping decorations, place it in the fridge to cool, before using.

Buttercream Ingredients
Butter

Buttercream recipes call for softened butter. What does this mean? Softened butter should keep shape when pressed down by a finger. Typically, depending on the temperature in your kitchen, it takes between thirty minutes to an hour to soften the butter. You can speed up the process by unwrapping and cutting the butter on pieces.

Sugar

Depending on a recipe, you will use either *powdered sugar* or *granulated sugar*. Granulated sugar is used in meringue-based buttercream recipes. These recipes require heating, and granulated sugar melts well when it is heated.

Powdered sugar is used in recipes that do not contain eggs. Powdered sugar mixed with butter creates a smooth consistency.

You should sift powdered sugar before mixing it with butter to prevent from creating lumps in your buttercream.

Do not use granulated sugar in non-meringue buttercream because you will feel sugar granules in the recipe.

It is best to use cane sugar (not beet sugar) to create the best texture and quality of buttercream.

Eggs

Some buttercream recipes call for using eggs when others do not require eggs. Meringue-based buttercreams make it easier to pipe complex shapes.

There is a way, however, to make eggless buttercream more stable and acceptable for piping. When you add cornstarch or corn flour, your buttercream becomes more stable.

Make sure to use organic corn starch and corn flour as corn products are likely to be genetically manipulated (GMO).

You can pasteurize raw eggs before you add them to a recipe.

To pasteurize eggs place a waterproof bowl into a saucepan. Add water to cover half of the bowl's height.

Place eggs into the bowl and heat the water up to 140°F. Let water boil for about three minutes to heat up the eggs. Do not let the water heat over 142°F.

Milk & Heavy Cream

When you are adding milk to buttercream, make sure it is whole milk. Whole milk contains a larger amount of fat. Alternatively, instead of adding milk you can add heavy cream.

Vanilla Extract

Vanilla enhances flavors. For instance, if the recipe uses chocolate, coffee, or fruit syrups, adding vanilla enhances the flavor of additives.

Vanilla extract comes in natural and artificial forms. A natural vanilla extract is superior to artificial vanilla extract. To create the best quality buttercream, use natural vanilla extract.

Almond Extract

The basic buttercream recipe does not call for using almond extract. Almond extract, however, enhances the taste.

The pure almond extract includes three primary ingredients: alcohol, water, and almond oil. To create the best quality buttercream and to add additional richness to your buttercream use natural almond extract.

Other ingredients

There are other ingredients that you can add to the buttercream. This includes fruit jellies, nuts, fresh fruits, nut butter and more.

American Buttercream

INGREDIENTS

8 Oz **Butter**, unsalted, softened

2 cups **Sugar**, powdered, sifted

2 tablespoons **Milk**

2 teaspoons **Vanilla**, pure, extract

EQUIPMENT

Stand or hand mixer fitted with the paddle attachment; Sifter; Food scale or measuring cups set; Cake decorating piping tips and bags (optional).

PREPARATION

Step 1: Place butter on a kitchen countertop and leave it until it reaches room temperature.

Step 2: In a bowl of stand mixer, fitted with the paddle attachment beat butter on medium speed for 2-3 minutes until it becomes soft and light.

Step 3: Gradually add one half of powdered sugar and beat starting on low speed and continuing on low-medium speed until fully incorporated.

Add vanilla extract. Beat again for 30 seconds.

Slowly add remaining sugar and beat on medium speed until all is fully incorporated and buttercream becomes light and fluffy. Do not overbeat.

Place into the fridge to cool.

Store in the refrigerator for up to one week. Beat it with a mixer before using.

Swiss Meringue Buttercream

INGREDIENTS

12 Oz **Butter**, unsalted, softened

1 cup **Sugar**, powdered, sifted

5 **Egg whites**

1 teaspoon **Vanilla**, pure, extract

¼ teaspoon **Salt**

EQUIPMENT

Stand or hand mixer fitted with the whisk attachment; Sifter; Heatproof bowl; Food scale or measuring cups set; Cake decorating piping tips and bags (optional).

PREPARATION

Step 1: Place butter on a kitchen countertop and leave it until it reaches room temperature.

Step 2: Place a heatproof bowl over low heat to create a slowly boiling water-bath.

Add egg whites and sugar into the water-bath bowl constantly stirring until sugar fully dissolves.

Step 3: Transfer the mixture into a bowl of stand mixer, fitted with the whisk attachment. Beat on medium speed for 4-5 minutes until meringue becomes thick and glossy.

Step 4: Add softened butter, salt, and vanilla and beat on medium speed until buttercream becomes silky and smooth.

Place into the fridge to cool.

Store in the refrigerator for up to one week. Beat it with a mixer before using.

German Buttercream

This buttercream is good for toppings. It also makes a good filling for pastries. It can be piped to decorate cakes and cupcakes as well.

INGREDIENTS

8 Oz **Butter**, unsalted, softened

1 cup **Sugar**, cane, granulated

3 **Egg yolks**, large, room temperature

¾ cup **Milk**, whole

1 tablespoon **Cornstarch,** organic (*or* **Corn** four)

1 teaspoon **Vanilla**, pure, extract

¼ teaspoon **Salt**

EQUIPMENT

Stand or hand mixer fitted with whisk and paddle attachments; Saucepan; Food scale or measuring cups set; Plastic wrap; Cake decorating piping tips and bags (optional).

PREPARATION

Step 1: Place butter on a kitchen countertop and leave it until it reaches room temperature.

Step 2: In a bowl of a stand mixer fitted with the paddle attachment, combine half of the granulated sugar, egg yolks, cornstarch, vanilla extract, and salt. Beat it until it becomes a bit foamy. Set it aside.

Step 3: In a saucepan, combine milk and second half of granulated sugar. Heat the mixture over medium-low heat, constantly stirring. Bring it to simmer, and remove from heat.

Step 4: Add half of the hot milk mixture into egg yolk mixture. Beat with the whisk attachment on low speed. Little by little add the rest of the hot milk mixture.

Step 5: Pour this mixture back into the saucepan, over medium-low heat. Stir constantly with a spatula until the mixture becomes a thick custard. Remove from heat once the mixture starts bubbling.

Step 6: Cover it with plastic wrap and place into the fridge to cool for approximately two hours.

Step 7: In a bowl of stand mixer, fitted with the paddle attachment, beat butter on medium speed for 2-3 minutes until it becomes soft and light.

Step 8: Add cooled custard mixture to the butter and beat on high speed with the paddle attachment until it becomes creamy and smooth. Do not overbeat.

Step 9: Add remaining powdered sugar, half of the key lime juice, and half of the milk. Process mixture until smooth.

For the best results use immediately.

Store it in the refrigerator for up to one week. Beat it with a mixer before using it for piping or decorating cakes.

French Buttercream

INGREDIENTS

16 oz **Butter**, unsalted, softened

8 **Egg yolks**, large, pasteurized

1 cup **Sugar**, cane, granulated

6 tablespoons **Water**

1 teaspoon **Vanilla**, pure, extract

Pinch of **Salt**

EQUIPMENT

Stand or hand mixer fitted with the whisk attachment; Medium saucepan; Sifter; Food scale or measuring cups set; Cake decorating piping tips and bags (optional).

PREPARATION

Step 1: Pasteurize egg yolks over the water-bath by bringing water to 140°F and simmer for about three minutes. Set aside to cool.

Step 2: Place cooled egg yolks into a bowl of a stand mixer equipped with the whisk attachment. Beat until it becomes thick and foamy.

Step 3: In a medium saucepan combine water and sugar. Heat the mixture over low-medium heat until sugar dissolves. Once sugar dissolves, increase the heat and bring the mixture to boil. Cook the mixture until it reaches 235°F. This will create hot syrup.

Step 4: Start adding the hot syrup into the mixing bowl of stand mixer, continuing mixing on low speed. Mix for 4-5 minutes until syrup cools down. Set aside to cool for another few minutes.

Step 5: Once the mixture cools down, add butter, one tablespoon at a time. Continue mixing on low speed until butter incorporates and the mixture looks creamy.

Add salt and vanilla and mix again for another 1-2 minutes until all is incorporated and becomes smooth and fluffy.

Place in the fridge to cool.

Store it in the refrigerator for up to one week. Beat it with a mixer before using it for piping or decorating cakes.

Italian Meringue Buttercream

This beautiful buttercream can withstand hot temperatures. This buttercream is perfect to stack tiered cakes (such as wedding cakes).

INGREDIENTS

1 ¼ cups **Sugar**, cane, granulated

2/3 cup **Maple syrup**

2/3 cup **Water**

5 **Egg whites**

1 1/3 cups **Butter,** unsalted, softened

2 2/3 cups **Shortening**, vegetable

2 teaspoons **Vanilla**, pure, extract

EQUIPMENT

Stand or hand mixer fitted with the paddle attachment; Medium heat-proof bowl; Candy thermometer;

Cake decorating piping tips and bags (optional).

PREPARATION

Step 1: In a heat-proof medium bowl combine sugar, maple syrup, and water. Bring to a boil over medium-high heat. Constantly stir the mixture and heat it to 223°F to and 234°F. Use candy thermometer to check the temperature.

The mixture is ready when it forms a soft thread when dripped from a spatula. This process should take between one and two minutes. Once it achieves the desired consistency remove it from heat and set aside.

Step 2: In a bowl of stand mixer fitted with the paddle attachment, add egg whites and beat on low and then on medium speed until it can hold a stiff peak.

Slowly pour sugar syrup mixture in a thin stream, while continuing to whip at a medium speed. Continue mixing for another 5-7 minutes. Set aside.

Step 3: One at a time, add pieces of cold butter. Continue to beat at medium speed until butter incorporates into the mixture.

Step 4: Add vegetable shortening and continue mixing at a medium speed.

The buttercream will break down and look crumbled. Keep mixing for another 10 minutes and it will become smooth and glossy.

Place into the fridge to cool.

Store it in the refrigerator for up to one week. Beat it with a mixer before using it for piping or decorating cakes.

This recipe contains raw egg. We recommend that pregnant women, young children, the elderly, and the infirm do not consume raw egg.

Morning Joy Coffee Buttercream

This coffee buttercream is a treat for coffee lovers. It works well with chocolate and caramel cakes.

INGREDIENTS

4 Oz **Butter**, unsalted, softened

2 cups **Sugar**, powdered

1 tablespoon **Cocoa powder**, unsweetened

1 tablespoon **Coffee**, strongly brewed

EQUIPMENT

Stand or hand mixer fitted with the paddle attachment; Whisk, Small mixing bowl; Cake decorating piping tips and bags (optional).

PREPARATION

Step 1: In a small mixing bowl whisk together powdered sugar and cocoa powder. Set aside.

Step 2: In a bowl of a stand mixer fitted with the paddle attachment add butter and beat it at medium speed for 3-4 minutes until creamy.

Gradually add sugar and cocoa powder mixture, and beat at medium speed for about 30 seconds. **Step 3:** Stir in the coffee, and beat until smooth for another 30 seconds. Do not overbeat.

Place into the fridge to cool.

Store it in the refrigerator for up to one week. Beat it with a mixer before using it for piping or decorating cakes.

QUICK AND SIMPLE BUTTERCREAM

This is a great "base" buttercream.

INGREDIENTS

4 Oz **Butter**, unsalted, softened

2 cups **Sugar**, powdered

2 tablespoons **Milk**

1 teaspoons **Vanilla**, pure, extract

1 teaspoons **Almond**, pure, extract

EQUIPMENT

Stand or hand mixer fitted with the paddle attachment; Cake decorating piping tips and bags (optional).

PREPARATION

Step 1: Place butter on a kitchen countertop and leave it until it reaches room temperature.

Step 2: In a bowl of stand mixer, fitted with the paddle attachment, add butter and beat it at medium speed until it becomes smooth and fluffy.

Step 3: Gradually add powdered sugar and beat until it is fully incorporated. Add vanilla and almond extracts and beat for another 30 seconds.

Step 4: Add milk and beat for another 30 to 45 seconds.

Place into the fridge to cool.

Store it in the refrigerator for up to one week. Beat it with a mixer before using it for piping or decorating cakes.

CREAM CHEESE DREAM BUTTERCREAM

Great buttercream for pumpkin bread, carrot cake and chocolate cake.

INGREDIENTS

16 Oz **Cream cheese**, softened

4 Oz **Butter**, unsalted, softened

4 cups **Sugar**, powdered

1 teaspoon **Vanilla**, pure, extract

EQUIPMENT

Stand or hand mixer fitted with the paddle attachment; Cake decorating piping tips and bags (optional).

PREPARATION

Step 1: Place butter and cream cheese on a kitchen countertop and leave it until it reaches room temperature.

Step 2: In a bowl of a stand mixer fitted with the paddle attachment add cream cheese and beat it at medium speed until it becomes smooth.

Little by little, add softened butter and continue mixing until it becomes smooth and fluffy.

Step 3: Add vanilla extract. Gradually add powdered sugar constantly beating on medium speed until all is fully incorporated and buttercream becomes light and fluffy.

Place into the fridge to cool.

Store it in the refrigerator for up to one week. Beat it with a mixer before using it for piping or decorating cakes.

DARK HORSE CHOCOLATE CREAM CHEESE BUTTERCREAM

This is a good buttercream for chocolate cakes decoration.

INGREDIENTS

16 Oz **Cream cheese**, softened

8 Oz **Butter**, unsalted, softened

2 cups **Sugar**, powdered

1/2 cup **Cocoa powder**, Dutch, unsweetened

1 teaspoon **Vanilla**, pure, extract

EQUIPMENT

Stand or hand mixer fitted with the paddle attachment; Medium mixing bowl; Cake decorating piping tips and bags (optional).

PREPARATION

Step 1: Place butter and cream cheese on a kitchen countertop and leave it until it reaches room temperature.

Step 2: In a medium mixing bowl combine powdered sugar and Dutch cocoa powder. Set aside.

Step 3: In a bowl of a stand mixer fitted with the paddle attachment add cream cheese and beat it at medium speed until mixture becomes smooth.

Little by little, add softened butter and continue mixing until it becomes smooth and fluffy.

Step 4: Add vanilla extract. Gradually add powdered sugar and cocoa powder. Mix by beating on medium speed until all is fully incorporated and buttercream becomes light and fluffy. Do not overbeat.

Place into the fridge to cool.

Store it in the refrigerator for up to one week. Beat it with a mixer before using it for piping or decorating cakes.

LEMON CREAM CHEESE BUTTERCREAM

This Lemon Cream Cheese Buttercream is good toping for lemon drops.

INGREDIENTS

4 Oz **Cream cheese**, softened

4 Oz **Butter**, unsalted, softened

2 ¼ cups **Sugar**, powdered *and*

1 cup **Sugar**, powdered

2 tablespoons **Lemon juice**

EQUIPMENT

Stand or hand mixer fitted with the paddle attachment; Medium mixing bowl; Cake decorating piping tips and bags (optional).

PREPARATION

Step 1: Place butter and cream cheese on a kitchen countertop and leave it until it reaches room temperature.

Step 2: In a medium mixing bowl combine powdered sugar and Dutch cocoa powder. Set aside.

Step 3: In a bowl of stand mixer fitted with the paddle attachment add cream cheese and beat it at medium speed until it becomes smooth.

Little by little, add softened butter and continue mixing until it becomes smooth and fluffy.

Step 4: Add one cup of powdered sugar and lemon juice. Beat until all is fully incorporated.

Step 5: Little by little, add the remaining two and one half cups of powdered sugar and mix until buttercream becomes creamy and light.

Place into the fridge to cool.

Store it in the refrigerator for up to one week. Beat it with a mixer before using it for piping or decorating cakes.

GERMAN CHOCOLATE BUTTERCREAM
Good buttercream for German Chocolate Cake.

INGREDIENTS

8 Oz **Butter**, softened

3 **Egg yolks**

1 1/3 cups **Coconut**, shredded, unsweetened

1 cup **Sugar**, brown

1 cup **Milk**, evaporated

1 cup **Pecans**, roasted, chopped

1 teaspoon **Vanilla**, pure, extract

EQUIPMENT

Stand or hand mixer fitted with the paddle attachment; Large saucepan; Cake decorating piping tips and bags (optional).

PREPARATION
Step 1: Place butter on a kitchen countertop and leave it until it reaches room temperature.

Step 2: In a large saucepan combine evaporated milk, brown sugar, egg yolks, butter, and vanilla. Cook the mixture over low heat constantly stirring until it thickens.

Remove from heat and stir in pecans and coconut. Set aside and let it cool to room temperature.

Step 3: In a bowl of a stand mixer fitted with the paddle attachment add softened butter and beat it at medium speed until it becomes smooth.

Step 4: Little by little, add cooled mixture and beat it on low to medium speed until all is incorporated and becomes smooth and fluffy.

Place into the fridge to cool.

Store it in the refrigerator for up to one week. Beat it with a mixer before using it for piping or decorating cakes.

Almond Buttercream

This buttercream is perfect for cookies and cupcakes.

INGREDIENTS

4 cups **Sugar**, white, powdered

1 cup **Butter**, unsalted, softened

1 cup **Shortening**, vegetable

4 1/2 tablespoons **Milk**

1 1/2 teaspoons **Almond**, extract, pure

EQUIPMENT

Stand or hand mixer fitted with the paddle attachment; Cake decorating piping tips and bags (optional).

PREPARATION

Step 1: Place butter on a kitchen countertop and leave it until it reaches room temperature.

Step 2: In a bowl of a stand mixer fitted with the paddle attachment combine softened butter and shortening. Beat it at medium speed for 3-4 minutes.

Add almond extract and beat for another 45 seconds.

Step 3: Add powdered sugar, one cup at a time. In between, add in milk, one tablespoon at a time. Mix for 30 seconds to 45 seconds until buttercream becomes creamy and smooth.

Place into the fridge to cool.

Store it in the refrigerator for up to one week. Beat it with a mixer before using it for piping or decorating cakes.

BANANA BUTTERCREAM

This buttercream is light and fluffy. It is good for decorating chocolate cakes and cupcakes.

INGREDIENTS

8 Oz **Whipped topping**, frozen, thawed

3.5 Oz **Banana pudding**, instant, mix

1 **Banana**, very ripe, mashed

1 cup **Milk**

2 tablespoons **Rum**

EQUIPMENT

Stand or hand mixer fitted with the paddle attachment; Cake decorating piping tips and bags (optional).

PREPARATION

Step 1: In a bowl of a stand mixer fitted with the paddle attachment combine banana pudding, mashed banana, milk, and rum.

Beat on a low to medium speed until mixture thickens.

Step 2: Gently beat in a thawed whipped topping. Continue to beat the mixture until it becomes smooth.

Place into the fridge to cool.

Store it in the refrigerator for up to one week. Beat it with a mixer before using it for piping or decorating cakes.

Paradise Island Buttercream

Perfect buttercream for cakes with condensed milk or chocolate cakes.

INGREDIENTS

2 cups **Sugar**, powdered

2 cups **Butter**, unsalted, softened

1 cup **Condensed milk**, sweetened

EQUIPMENT

Stand or hand mixer fitted with the paddle attachment; Cake decorating piping tips and bags (optional).

PREPARATION

Step 1: Place butter on a kitchen countertop and leave it until it reaches room temperature.

Step 2: In a bowl of stand mixer fitted with the paddle attachment beat softened butter at medium speed, until it becomes smooth and fluffy.

Step 3: Gradually beat in powdered sugar until it becomes fully incorporated.

Step 4: Add condensed milk, continue to beat until the mixture becomes smooth.

Place in the fridge to cool.

Store it in the refrigerator for up to one week. Beat it with a mixer before using it for piping or decorating cakes.

SILVER MOUNTAIN BUTTERCREAM
This is a very good frosting for any kind of cakes.

INGREDIENTS

3 cups **Sugar**, cane, powdered

3 **Egg whites**

1 cup **Water**

1/4 teaspoon **Cream of tartar**

1 teaspoon **Vanilla**, pure, extract

EQUIPMENT

Stand or hand mixer fitted with the paddle attachment; Large saucepan; Candy thermometer; Cake decorating piping tips and bags (optional).

PREPARATION

Step 1: In a large saucepan combine sugar, water, and cream of tartar. Cook until it reaches 238°F (measure with a candy thermometer), or until syrup spins a long thread when it is dripped from a spatula.

Set aside to cool slightly.

Step 2: In a bowl of a stand mixer, fitted with the paddle attachment, beat egg whites until they start to firm up.

Step 3: Pour a slow stream of syrup into egg whites, beating constantly, until frosting stands in peaks.

Add in vanilla extract and beat for another 30 – 45 seconds.

Place in the fridge to cool.

Store it in the refrigerator for up to one week. Beat it with a mixer before using it for piping or decorating cakes.

This recipe contains raw egg. We recommend that pregnant women, young children, the elderly, and the infirm do not consume raw egg.

Unbaked Meringue Icing

This meringue is amazingly creamy and fluffy.

INGREDIENTS

2 **Egg whites**

1/4 cup **Sugar**, cane, powdered

1/4 cup **Maple syrup**

3 tablespoons **Water**

1/8 teaspoon **Cream of tartar**

1/4 teaspoon **Salt**

EQUIPMENT

Stand or hand mixer fitted with the paddle attachment; Medium saucepan; Candy thermometer; Cake decorating piping tips and bags (optional).

PREPARATION

Step 1: In a medium saucepan, combine sugar, maple syrup, water, cream of tartar, and salt. Cook over medium heat, constantly stirring until mixture comes to a boil and sugar dissolves. Remove from heat. Cool to lukewarm (110°F).

Step 2: In a bowl of stand mixer, fitted with the paddle attachment, beat egg whites on medium speed until foamy.

Slowly pour the lukewarm syrup and beat it on high speed until it starts to form stiff peaks.

If you desire to achieve brown color meringue, place it into the oven and bake until it gets brown.

Place into the fridge to cool.

Store it in the refrigerator for up to one week. Beat it with a mixer before using it for piping or decorating cakes.

This recipe contains raw egg. We recommend that pregnant women, young children, the elderly, and the infirm do not consume raw egg.

MARZIPAN ICING

Marzipan Icing is great for Christmas cakes and candies.

INGREDIENTS

2 cups **Sugar**, white, powdered

1/2 pound **Almonds**, blanched, finely ground

2 **Egg whites,** pasteurized

1/2 teaspoon **Salt,** sea salt

1/2 teaspoon **Almond**, extract, pure

EQUIPMENT

Stand or hand mixer fitted with the paddle attachment; Plastic wrap.

PREPARATION

Step 1: In a bowl of stand mixer, fitted with the paddle attachment, combine, powdered sugar and egg whites. Beat on medium speed until mixture becomes smooth and foamy.

Step 2: Add finely ground almonds, salt, and almond extract. Beat on medium speed until all is perfectly blended.

Cover with plastic wrap and leave in the fridge for 24 hours to harden.

Store it in the refrigerator for up to one week

This recipe contains raw egg. We recommend that pregnant women, young children, the elderly, and the infirm do not consume raw egg.

Caramel Dreams Buttercream

This caramel buttercream is wonderful for chocolate cakes.

INGREDIENTS

1 cup **Sugar**, brown

1/3 cup **Milk,** whole

2 tablespoons **Butter**, unsalted, softened

1 tablespoon **Cream**, heavy

1 teaspoon **Vanilla**, pure, extract

1/8 teaspoon **Salt**

EQUIPMENT

Stand or hand mixer fitted with the paddle attachment; Large saucepan; Cake decorating piping tips and bags (optional).

PREPARATION

Step 1: In a large saucepan, combine brown sugar, salt, butter, and milk. Cook over medium heat constantly stirring until mixture comes to a boil and sugar has dissolved.

Cool to lukewarm (110 F).

Step 2: Transfer the mixture into a bowl of a stand mixer fitted with the paddle attachment and beat for 7-10 minutes until it begins to thicken.

Add vanilla and heavy cream and beat for another 1-2 minutes until frosting becomes smooth.

Place into the fridge to cool.

Store it in the refrigerator for up to one week. Beat it with a mixer before using it for piping or decorating cakes.

Go Nuts Cream Cheese Buttercream

This is a great nut-flavored buttercream for chocolate cakes.

INGREDIENTS

8 Oz **Cream cheese**, softened

4 Oz **Butter**, unsalted, softened

4 cups **Sugar**, powdered

1 cup **Pecans**, chopped

EQUIPMENT

Stand or hand mixer fitted with the paddle attachment; Cake decorating piping tips and bags (optional).

PREPARATION

Step 1: Place butter and cream cheese on a kitchen countertop and leave it until it reaches room temperature.

Step 2: In a bowl of stand mixer, fitted with the paddle attachment, beat cream cheese on medium speed for 3-4 minutes until it becomes soft and fluffy.

Step 3: Little by little, add softened butter and beat on medium speed until all is incorporated and fluffy.

Step 4: Add powdered sugar and vanilla. Beat until creamy and add chopped nuts. Mix for another 45 seconds.

Place into the fridge to cool.

Store it in the refrigerator for up to one week. Beat it with a mixer before using it for piping or decorating cakes.

Strawberry Cream Cheese Frosting

Good buttercream for many kinds of cakes including chocolate or white cakes.

INGREDIENTS

4 Oz **Cream cheese**, softened

4 Oz **Butter**, unsalted, softened

1 1/4 cups **Sugar**, powdered

1/2 cup **Cream**, heavy whipping

1/4 cup **Strawberry**, puree

1/2 teaspoon **Vanilla**, pure extract

EQUIPMENT

Stand or hand mixer fitted with the paddle attachment; Cake decorating piping tips and bags (optional).

PREPARATION

Step 1: Place butter and cream cheese on a kitchen countertop and leave it until it reaches room temperature.

Step 2: Chill a large glass or a metal bowl and the beaters in the freezer for 30 minutes.

Step 3: In a chilled bowl of a stand mixer add heavy whipping cream. Beat it on medium speed for 5-6 minutes until stiff peaks start to form.

Step 4: In a separate bowl beat cream cheese for 1-2 minutes until it becomes creamy.

Step 5: Add softened butter and continue beating on medium speed for 3-4 minutes until it becomes well blended and smooth.

Step 6: Add strawberry puree and vanilla extract. Beat for another 2-3 minutes. Add powdered sugar and beat for 4-5 minutes until it is soft and fluffy.

Step 7: Fold in the whipped cream into the cream cheese mixture until whipped cream is evenly incorporated.

Place into the fridge to cool.

Store it in the refrigerator for up to one week. Beat it with a mixer before using it for piping or decorating cakes.

Hazelnut Buttercream

This frosting is wonderful for chocolate cakes.

INGREDIENTS

8 Oz **Cream cheese**, softened

4 Oz cup **Butter**, unsalted, softened

1 cup **Chocolate-hazelnut**, spread

1 tablespoon **Milk**

EQUIPMENT

Stand or hand mixer fitted with the paddle attachment; Cake decorating piping tips and bags (optional).

PREPARATION

Step 1: Place butter and cream cheese on a kitchen countertop and leave it until it reaches room temperature.

Step 2: In a bowl of stand mixer, fitted with the paddle attachment, beat cream cheese on medium speed for 4-5 minutes until it becomes soft and fluffy.

Step 3: Little by little add softened butter and beat on medium speed until all is incorporated and fluffy.

Step 4: Add hazelnut spread and milk and continue beating until smooth and fluffy.

Place into the fridge to cool.

Store it in the refrigerator for up to one week. Beat it with a mixer before using it for piping or decorating cakes.

AMARETTO-MAPLE CREAM CHEESE BUTTERCREAM

Good buttercream for many kinds of cakes, including, chocolate cakes.

INGREDIENTS

8 Oz cream cheese, softened

4 Oz **Butter**, unsalted, softened

2 ½ cups Sugar, powdered

1/4 cup **Amaretto liqueur**

1 tablespoon **Maple syrup**, pure

1/2 teaspoon **Vanilla**, pure, extract

EQUIPMENT

Stand or hand mixer fitted with the paddle attachment; Cake decorating piping tips and bags (optional).

PREPARATION

Step 1: Place butter and cream cheese on a kitchen countertop and leave it until it reaches room temperature.

Step 2: In a bowl of stand mixer, fitted with the paddle attachment, beat cream cheese on medium speed for 5-7 minutes until it becomes soft and fluffy.

Step 3: Little by little, add softened butter and beat on medium speed until all is incorporated and fluffy.

Step 4: Add powdered sugar, amaretto liqueur, maple syrup, and vanilla extract. Beat it for another 1-2 minutes until smooth and fluffy.

Place into the fridge to cool.

Store it in the refrigerator for up to one week. Beat it with a mixer before using it for piping or decorating cakes.

Chocolate Marshmallow Fondant
Very good chocolate fondant to cover chocolate cakes.

INGREDIENTS

16 Oz **Marshmallow**s, miniature

4 cups **Sugar**, powdered

1/2 cup **Chocolate chips**, dark, bakers

2 tablespoons **Maple syrup**

1 teaspoon **Coffee**, extract

EQUIPMENT

Two small heat proof bowls. Plastic wrap.

PREPARATION

Step 1: In a small bowl melt marshmallows constantly stirring, on a water-bath.

Add maple syrup and coffee-flavored extract.

Step 2: In a small bowl melt chocolate chips constantly stirring, on a water bath.

Step 3. Fold in chocolate mixture into the marshmallow mixture.

Step 4: Add powdered sugar, one cup at a time, into the chocolate-marshmallow mixture, until a thick, stringy dough forms.

Step 5: Add some powdered sugar on a flat working surface; turn dough out and knead until smooth and no longer sticky.

Step 6: Wrap tightly in plastic wrap. Let fondant rest at room temperature, from eight hours to overnight.

Store in the refrigerator for up to one week.

SNOW WHITE BUTTERCREAM

This simple buttercream is good for any kind of cupcakes or cakes.

INGREDIENTS

1 cup **Sugar**, cane, powdered

1/2 cup **Butter**, unsalted, softened

1/2 cup **Shortening**, vegetable

1/4 cup **Flour**, all-purpose

1 cup **Milk**

1 teaspoon **Vanilla**, pure, extract

EQUIPMENT

Stand or hand mixer fitted with the paddle attachment; Small saucepan, Cake decorating piping tips and bags (optional).

PREPARATION

Step 1: In a small saucepan, combine milk and flour. Cook over medium-high heat until mixture is boiling. Remove from heat and set aside to cool.

Step 2: In a bowl of a stand mixer, fitted with the paddle attachment, beat softened butter on medium speed for 3-4 minutes until it becomes soft and fluffy. Slowly add powdered sugar and beat on slow speed until all is fully incorporated.

Step 3: Add vegetable shortening and vanilla. Beat on medium speed for one minute.

Step 4: Transfer the cooled mixture into the bowl with buttercream. Beat it on medium speed until all is fully incorporated.

Place into the fridge to cool.

Store it in the refrigerator for up to one week. Beat it with a mixer before using it for piping or decorating cakes.

CHRISTMAS EGGNOG BUTTERCREAM

This is a great buttercream to decorate holiday cakes and cupcakes.

INGREDIENTS

4 cups **Sugar**, powdered

4 Oz **Butter**, unsalted, softened

6 tablespoons **Eggnog**

1 teaspoon **Vanilla**, pure, extract

EQUIPMENT

Stand or hand mixer fitted with the paddle attachment; Cake decorating piping tips and bags (optional).

PREPARATION

Step 1: Place butter on a kitchen countertop and leave it until it reaches room temperature.

Step 2: In a bowl of stand mixer, fitted with the paddle attachment, beat butter on medium speed for 3-4 minutes until it becomes soft and light.

Step 3: Add eggnog and vanilla extract. Beat on medium speed until all is well combined.

Step 4: Slowly add powdered sugar. Keep beating until the mixture becomes soft and fluffy.

Place into the fridge to cool.

Store it in the refrigerator for up to one week. Beat it with a mixer before using it for piping or decorating cakes.

Raspberry Buttercream

Perfect buttercream for any cake that calls for a fruity flavor.

INGREDIENTS

For the Buttercream:

2 cups **Sugar**, powdered

1 cup **Butter**, unsalted, softened

1 teaspoon **Vanilla**, pure, extract

For the Raspberry Puree:

1 cup **Raspberries**, fresh or frozen, thawed

2 tablespoons **Cream,** heavy, whipping

EQUIPMENT

Stand or hand mixer fitted with the paddle attachment; Blender; Small saucepan; Cake decorating piping tips and bags (optional).

PREPARATION

Make the Puree:

Step 1: In a blender puree raspberries and heavy cream until smooth.

Transfer into a small saucepan, add two tablespoons of powdered sugar and reduce the liquid by simmering over low heat. Set aside to cool.

Make the Buttercream:

Step 1: Place butter and on a kitchen countertop and leave it until it reaches room temperature.

Step 2: In a bowl of stand mixer, fitted with the paddle attachment, beat butter on medium speed for 3-4 minutes until it becomes soft and light.

Step 3: Gradually add powdered sugar and beat until fully incorporated. Add vanilla extract and beat again for 30 seconds.

Step 4: Add raspberry puree and beat for another 45 seconds. Do not overbeat.

Place into the fridge to cool.

Store it in the refrigerator for up to one week. Beat it with a mixer before using it for piping or decorating cakes.

BONUS RECIPES

BLACK VOLCANO BUTTERCREAM

Great buttercream icing for chocolate or caramel cakes.

INGREDIENTS

12 Oz **Condensed milk**, sweetened

8 Oz **Butter**, unsalted, softened

2 cups **Sugar**, powdered

1/2 cup **Cocoa powder**, Dutch, unsweetened

1 teaspoon **Vanilla**, pure, extract

EQUIPMENT

Stand or hand mixer fitted with the paddle attachment; Cake decorating piping tips and bags (optional).

PREPARATION

Step 1: Place butter and on a kitchen countertop and leave it until it reaches room temperature.

Step 2: In a bowl of stand mixer, fitted with the paddle attachment, beat butter on medium speed, for 3-4 minutes until it becomes soft and light.

Step 3: Gradually add powdered sugar and beat until fully incorporated. Add vanilla extract and beat again for 30 seconds.

Step 4: Add condensed milk and cocoa powder and beat until smooth. Do not overbeat.

Place into the fridge to cool.

Store it in the refrigerator for up to one week. Beat it with a mixer before using it for piping or decorating cakes.

Avocado Buttercream

This is a lighter version of buttercream. Great for carrot cupcakes.

INGREDIENTS

2 cups **Sugar**, powdered

8 Oz **Avocado**, meat of *(approx. 2 avocados)*

2 teaspoons **Lemon juice**, freshly squeezed

1/2 teaspoon **Lemon**, extract

EQUIPMENT

Stand or hand mixer fitted with the paddle attachment; Cake decorating piping tips and bags (optional).

PREPARATION

Step 1: Peel and pit the avocados. Place avocado meat into a bowl of a stand mixer, add lemon juice and beat for 2 to 3 minutes until it lightens in color.

Step 2: Add powdered sugar (little at a time) and beat until smooth. Add the lemon extract and beat for another 30 seconds to combine.

Place into the fridge to cool.

Store in the refrigerator for up to 1 week. Beat it with a mixer before using.

CHAMPAGNE BUTTERCREAM

Surprise your guests with champagne buttercream decorated cakes or cupcakes.

INGREDIENTS

8 Oz **butter**, unsalted, softened

3 cups **Sugar**, powdered

4 tablespoons **Champagne**

EQUIPMENT

Stand or hand mixer fitted with the paddle attachment; Cake decorating piping tips and bags (optional).

PREPARATION

Step 1: Place butter and on a kitchen countertop and leave it until it reaches room temperature.

Step 2: In a bowl of stand mixer, fitted with the paddle attachment, beat butter on medium speed for 3-4 minutes until it becomes soft and light.

Step 3: Gradually add powdered sugar and beat until it is fully incorporated. Add vanilla extract and beat again for 30 seconds.

Step 4: Add Champagne and mix until it is evenly incorporated and the frosting is smooth and creamy.

Place into the fridge to cool.

Store in the refrigerator for up to 1 week. Beat it with a mixer before using.

CHOCOLATE CAKE PRAGUE

This cake is tasty and easy to make. Make it for the holidays and surprise your guests and loved ones.

INGREDIENTS

For the Cake:

2 cups **Flour**, white, all-purpose

1 cup **Sugar**

6 **Eggs**

14 Oz **Condensed Milk**, sweetened

1 cup **Buttermilk** (or sour cream), room temperature

1 cup **Cocoa powder**, unsweetened

1 teaspoon **Baking powder**

3/4 teaspoon **Baking soda**

1/2 teaspoon **Lemon**, juice of

1/4 teaspoon **Salt,** sea salt

1/3 cup **Vegetable oil,** olive, virgin

1 teaspoon **Vanilla,** extract, pure

Cooking spray for greasing the pans

For the Frosting:

12 Oz **Butter**, unsalted, softened

2 cups **Sugar**, powdered

14 Oz **Condensed Milk**, sweetened

1/2 cup **Cocoa powder**, unsweetened

1 teaspoon **Vanilla,** extract, pure

1 teaspoon **Rum** (optional)

Equipment:

Two (9-inch-round, 2-inch-deep) cake pans or one (9- by 13-inch) baking pan; Stand or hand mixer fitted with the paddle attachment; large mixing bowl, 1 to 2 wire cooling racks; Spatula or cake scraper; Cake decorating piping tips and bags (optional), rotating cake table (optional); Parchment paper (optional).

PREPARATION

Make the Cake:

Step 1: Preheat oven to 355°F. With the cooking spray, grease the bottom and sides of 2 (9-inch-round, 2-inch-deep) cake pans. Line the bottoms with parchment paper (optional).

Step 2: In a large bowl, sift and combine flour, cocoa powder, baking powder, baking soda, and salt.

Step 3: In a bowl of stand mixer fitted with the paddle attachment (you can use a bowl and a hand mixer) combine sugar and eggs.

Beat on low to medium speed until everything is well incorporated and achieves a smooth consistency.

Add buttermilk (or sour cream) and continue mixing until all is well incorporated.

Add vegetable oil, vanilla extract, and lemon juice. Continue mixing for another 2-3 minutes.

Step 4: Separate dry flour mix on 3 or 4 parts and add it to the wet mixture in 3 or 4 batches. Beat at low speed to incorporate.

Once all is incorporated, beat on medium speed for another 1-2 minutes. If you see the mixture is too dry, add more buttermilk or milk (little at a time).

Step 5: Separate the batter into two equal parts and spread between the two greased pans. Bake until firm for about 25 - 30 minutes or until wooden skewer tester comes out clean.

Step 6: Transfer crusts onto the cooling racks and peel off the parchment paper (if you are using it). Let the cake cool completely.

Make the Frosting:

Step 1: In a bowl of stand mixer fitted with the paddle attachment (you can use a bowl and a hand mixer) combine butter and powdered sugar.

Beat on medium speed for 2 to 3 minutes until it is fully incorporated and becomes fluffy and light in color.

Add vanilla extract and beat for another 1-2 minutes.

If you would like to decorate your cake set aside and refrigerate 1/3 of the frosting for about an hour until it becomes firm.

Step 2: Little at a time add condensed milk and beat on medium speed for to 3-5 minutes until it is fully incorporated.

Assemble the Cake:

If you would like to decorate your cake set aside and refrigerate 1/3 of the frosting for about an hour until it becomes firm.

This will be your "cooled frosting". The rest of the frosting will be "room temperature" frosting.

Step 1: If you set aside 1/3 of the frosting for cake decorating, divide the rest of the room temperature frosting into three equal parts.

(If not, divide the entire amount of yielded frosting into three equal parts).

Place a small portion (1-2 tablespoons) of frosting on top of the serving plate.

Step 2: Place the first cake layer on the serving plate and cover top of the crust with 1/3 of room temperature frosting.

Step 3: Place the second layer on top and cover it with 1/3 of room temperature frosting.

Step 4: Use the remaining 1/3 of room temperature frosting to spread on sides of the cake. Level the edges and surface of the cake with a spatula or a scraper. Place it into the fridge to cool.

Use cooled frosting to decorate the cooled cake using piping tips and bags. (Optional).

Decorate the Cake: (optional)

Once you are ready to decorate your cake using piping tips and bags, remove the cooled frosting from the fridge.

Place the cooled frosting into a piping bag and start piping borders and flowers. You can also add food coloring. *(We recommend using natural food coloring instead of artificial colors).*

Store in the refrigerator for up to 5 days or in the fridge for up to one month.

Black Forest Meringue Chocolate Cake

INGREDIENTS

For the Cake:

2 cups **Flour**, white, all-purpose

1 ½ cups **Sugar,** white, granulated

1 cup **Sugar**, brown

4 **Eggs**

1 cup **Buttermilk** (or sour cream), room temperature

1 cup **Cocoa powder**, Dutch, unsweetened

1/2 cup **Chocolate,** baking, dark

1 teaspoon **Baking powder**

3/4 teaspoon **Baking soda**

1/2 teaspoon **Lemon**, juice of

1/4 teaspoon **Salt,** sea salt

3/4 cup **Vegetable oil,** olive, virgin

1 teaspoon **Vanilla**, extract, pure

Cooking spray for greasing the pans

For the Meringue:

4 **Egg**, whites, room temperature

1 cup **Sugar**

1/3 teaspoon **Cream of tartar**

1 teaspoon **Vanilla**, extract, pure

For the Filling:

24 Oz **Sour cherries,** pitted (or **Tart** cherries), pitted

1 cup **Sugar,** white, refined

1/4 cup **Cornstarch**, organic

1/2 tablespoon **Vanilla,** extract, pure

For the Frosting:

2 ½ cups **Heavy whipping cream**

3 cups **Sugar**, powdered

1 tablespoon **Vanilla,** extract, pure

For the Buttercream: (optional)

8 Oz **Butter**, unsalted, softened

4 cups **Sugar**, powdered

1 teaspoon **Vanilla**, extract, pure

Equipment:

Two (9-inch-round, 2-inch-deep) cake pans or One (9- by 13-inch) baking pan; Medium size saucepan, Large and small baking trays, Stand or hand mixer fitted with the paddle attachment; Large mixing bowl, 1 to 2 wire cooling racks; Spatula or cake scraper; Cake decorating piping tips and bags (optional), rotating cake table (optional).

PREPARATION

Make the Meringue:

Preheat oven to 250°F.

Step 1: In a bowl of stand mixer fitted with the paddle attachment (you can use a bowl and a hand mixer) combine egg whites, cream of tartar, and vanilla. Beat on medium speed until foamy.

One spoon at a time, add sugar and beat the mixture until sugar dissolves, then add more sugar.

Repeat.

Continue beating for 7 to 10 minutes until still glossy peaks start forming.

Step 2: Take your pastry bag and set a decorating tip with a small hole. Alternatively, you can cut a small hole in the pastry piping bag.

Step 3: Transfer meringue into the piping bag. Pipe 1.5 – 2-inch diameter cookies onto a large baking tray lined with parchment paper. Space them two inches apart.

On a small baking tray lined up with a parchment paper, pipe smaller cookies (0.5 inches) for cake decorations. Space them one inch apart.

Step 4: Bake meringues on a large tray for 40-45 minutes or until they become firm. After twenty minutes of baking, add the small tray with meringues into the oven.

Bake for another 25 minutes or until firm to touch. Turn off oven and leave meringues in oven for about one hour.

Step 5: Remove meringues from the oven, separate from the parchment paper. Set aside small meringues for cake decorations.

Turn large meringues into crumbs of approximately 1/4 inch in size. Set aside.

Make the Cake:

Step 1: Preheat oven to 355°F. With the cooking spray, grease the bottom and sides of two (9-inch-round, 2-inch-deep) cake pans. Line the bottoms with parchment paper (optional).

Step 2: In a large bowl, sift and combine flour, cocoa powder, baking powder, baking soda, and salt.

Step 3: In a bowl of stand mixer fitted with the paddle attachment (you can use a bowl and a hand mixer) combine sugar, brown sugar, and eggs.

Beat on low to medium speed until everything is well incorporated and achieves a smooth consistency.

Add buttermilk (or sour cream) and continue mixing until all is well incorporated.

Add vegetable oil, pure vanilla extract, and lemon juice. Continue mixing for another 2-3 minutes.

Step 4: Separate dry flour mix on 3 or 4 parts and add it to the wet mixture in 3 or 4 batches while beating at low speed to incorporate.

Once all is incorporated, beat on medium speed for another 1-2 minutes. If you see the mixture is too dry, add more buttermilk or milk (little at a time).

Step 5: Separate batter into two parts and spread evenly between two greased bowls. Bake until firm for about 25 - 30 minutes or until wooden skewer tester comes clean.

Step 6: Transfer crusts onto the cooling racks and peel off the parchment paper (if you are using it). Let the cake cool completely.

Make the Filling:

Step 1: Drain the cherries, reserve and set aside the cherry juice. In a medium-size saucepan add drained tart cherries, sugar, cornstarch, 1/2 cup of the reserved cherry juice, and vanilla extract. Whisk all together.

Step 2: Cook over low heat constantly stirring for about 10 minutes or until the mixture thickens. Set aside to cool.

Make the Frosting:

Step 1: In a bowl of stand mixer fitted with the paddle attachment (you can use a bowl and a hand mixer) combine heavy whipping cream, powdered sugar, and vanilla extract. Beat on medium speed until it becomes light and fluffy.

Make the Buttercream:

Step 1: In a bowl of stand mixer fitted with the paddle attachment (you can use a bowl and a hand mixer) combine butter and powdered sugar.

Beat on medium speed for 2 to 3 minutes until it is fully incorporated and becomes fluffy and light in color.

Add vanilla extract and beat for another 1-2 minutes. Refrigerate for about one hour until it becomes firm.

Assemble the Cake:

Step 1: Place a small portion (1-2 tablespoons) of frosting on top of the serving plate.

Step 2: Cut cooled crusts with a knife or cake cutting tool into two pieces. You will have four cake layers.

Step 3: Place the first cake layer on the serving plate and cover top of the crust with 1/4 of the cherry filling. Place 1/4 of meringue crumbs on top of the cherry filling. Cover meringue crumbs with 1/4 of the frosting.

Step 4: Place the second cake layer on top and cover it with 1/4 of the cherry filling. Place 1/4 of meringue crumbs on top of the cherry filling. Cover meringue crumbs with 1/4 of the frosting.

Step 5: Place the third cake layer on top and cover it with 1/4 of the cherry filling. Place 1/4 of meringue crumbs on top of the cherry filling. Cover meringue crumbs with 1/4 of the frosting.

Step 6: Place the fourth cake layer on top and cover it with 1/4 of the cherry filling. Place 1/4 of meringue crumbs on top of the cherry filling. Cover meringue crumbs with 1/4 of the frosting. Level the edges and surface of the cake with a spatula or a scraper.

Decorate the Cake:

Option 1: Decorate top of the cake with cherries and reserved small meringue cookies.

Option 2: Create cake decorations using cake decorating tools: piping tips and bags.

For Option 2 you will need to create buttercream.

Before you decorate the cake cool your cake and buttercream in the fridge.

Once you are ready to decorate your cake using piping tips and bags, remove the cooled cake and buttercream from the fridge.

Place the cooled buttercream into a piping bag and start piping borders and flowers. You can also add food coloring. *(We recommend using natural food coloring instead of artificial colors).*

Add cherries and small meringue cookies as part of your cake decorating design.

Store in the refrigerator for up to 5 days or in the fridge for up to one month.

White Chocolate Raspberry Cheesecake

INGREDIENTS

For the Cake:

1 ½ cups **Flour**, all-purpose

1 cup **Sugar,** white, granulated

1/2 cup **Sugar**, brown

6 **Eggs**

1 cup **Chocolate chips,** white, bakers

1/2 cup **Applesauce,** unsweetened

1/2 cup **Buttermilk**

1 teaspoon **Baking powder**

3/4 teaspoon **Baking soda**

3/4 teaspoon **Salt**

1 cup **Vegetable oil**

Cooking spray for greasing the springform pan

For the Syrup:

1/2 cup **Raspberry preserve**, seedless

6 tablespoons **Water**

For the Cheese:

8 Oz **Cream cheese**

1 **Egg**

1/4 cup **Buttermilk**

1/4 cup **Sour cream**

1 tablespoon **Flour,** all purpose

For the Frosting:

6 Oz **Farmer cheese**

6 Oz **Butter**, unsalted, softened

2 ½ cups **Sugar**, powdered

1/2 tablespoon **Vanilla,** extract

For the Decorations:

1 cup **Coconut**, unsweetened, shredded

EQUIPMENT

One 9-inch springform baking pan; Small saucepan; Stand or hand mixer fitted with the paddle attachment; Small, medium and large mixing bowls, Spatula or cake scraper; Cake decorating piping tips and bags (optional).

PREPARATION

Make the Cake:

Step 1: Preheat oven to 355°F. Grease the bottom and sides of 9-inch springform pan with the cooking spray.

Line the bottom of the pan with parchment paper (optional).

Step 2: In a large bowl, sift and combine flour, baking powder, baking soda, and salt. Add white chocolate chips. Set aside.

Step 3: In a bowl of stand mixer fitted with the paddle attachment (you can use a bowl and a hand mixer) combine sugar and eggs.

Mix on low speed until everything is well incorporated and achieves a smooth consistency.

Add vegetable oil, buttermilk, vanilla, and applesauce. Continue mixing until all is well incorporated.

Step 4: Separate flour mix (from Step 2) onto three or four parts and add it in three or four batches. Use a spatula to fold the mixture together until all is incorporated. Set aside.

Make the Syrup:

Step 1: In a small saucepan combine raspberry preserves and water. Warm up on low heat constantly mixing until it melts.

Make the Cheese:

Step 1: Combine cream cheese, buttermilk, sour cream, and flour. Beat the mixture with a paddle attachment until all is evenly incorporated and mixture becomes smooth.

Step 2: Fold in raspberry syrup. Gently mix with a spatula. Do not over mix.

Assemble the Cake:

Step 1: Pour 1/3 of cake batter into greased springform pan.

Pour 1/3 of raspberry cheese over the cake batter.

Step 2: Repeat to add all batter and raspberry cheese into the springform pan.

Bake the Cake:

Preheat oven to 355F. Bake the cake for about 60-65 minutes or until the center is set and not very wobbly. At 30-35 minutes into baking, cover the springform with aluminum foil to prevent burning of the top of the cake.

Once ready set it aside for an hour to cool. (Preferably leave it overnight in the fridge once it is cool).

Make the Frosting:

Step 1: In a bowl of stand mixer fitted with the paddle attachment (you can use a bowl and a hand mixer) combine butter and powdered sugar.

Beat on medium speed for 2 to 3 minutes until it is fully incorporated and becomes fluffy and light in color.

Step 2: Spoon by spoon, add farmers cheese and beat on medium speed for 2 to 3 minutes until it is fully incorporated and becomes light and fluffy.

Add vanilla extract and beat for another 2-3 minutes.

If you decorate your cake: set aside and refrigerate 1/3 of the frosting for about an hour until it gets firm.

Step 3: Spread the room temperature frosting over the cake. Level the edges and surface with a spatula or scraper.

Use cooled frosting to decorate the cake using piping tips and bags. (Optional).

Decorate the Cake:

Cover top of cheesecake with frosting. Sprinkle with shredded coconut.

Once you are ready to decorate your cake remove the cooled frosting from the fridge.

Place the cooled frosting into a piping bag and start piping borders and flowers. You can also add food coloring. *(We recommend using natural food coloring instead of artificial colors).*

Store in the refrigerator for up to 5 days or in the fridge for up to one month.

TROPICAL PARADISE CARROT CAKE
INGREDIENTS

For the Crust:

1 lbs. **Carrots**, peeled

4 **Eggs**

2 cups **Flour**, all-purpose

1 cup **Sugar,** cane, granulated

1 cup **Sugar**, brown

1 teaspoon **Baking Powder**

3/4 teaspoon **Baking Soda**

3/4 teaspoon **Salt,** sea, fine

1 cup **Olive Oil,** cold pressed, virgin

1/2 cup **Walnuts,** raw, chopped

1/2 cup **Pineapple,** dried, diced

1/2 cup **Raisins**, dark

1/2 cup **Apricots**, dried, diced

1 teaspoons **Cinnamon**, ground

1/2 teaspoon **Nutmeg**, grated

Cooking spray for greasing the pans

For the Frosting:

8 Oz **Cream Cheese**, room temperature

8 Oz **Farmer Cheese** (optional, or use 16 Oz cream cheese if you are not using cream cheese)

8 Oz **Butter**, unsalted, softened

3 cups **Sugar**, powdered

1 tablespoon **Vanilla,** extract

1/2 cup **Apricot Jam** (optional)

EQUIPMENT

Two (9-inch-round, 2-inch-deep) cake pans or one (9- by 13-inch) baking pan, Stand or hand mixer fitted with the paddle attachment, Small, medium and large mixing bowls, One or two wire cooling racks, Food processor equipped with S-blade or hand grater, Cake decorating piping tips and bags (optional).

PREPARATION

Make the Crusts:

Step 1: Preheat oven to 355°F. With the cooking spray, grease the bottom and sides of two (9-inch-round, 2-inch-deep) cake pans. Line the bottoms with parchment paper (optional).

Step 2: Grate the carrots in a food processor (or with a hand grater). Grate walnuts in a food processor (or with a hand grater).

In a medium bowl, combine carrots and walnuts. Add raisins.

Step 3: Dice dried fruits into 1/2-inch pieces. In a small bowl, combine diced pineapple and apricot. Add one cup of water and leave for about 1 hour to soften.

Step 4: In a large bowl, combine flour, baking powder, baking soda, salt, cinnamon, and nutmeg.

Step 5: In a bowl of stand mixer fitted with the paddle attachment (you can use a bowl and a hand mixer) add sugar, brown sugar, and eggs.

Mix on low speed until everything is well incorporated and achieves a smooth consistency.

Add vegetable oil and continue mixing until all is well incorporated.

Step 6: Separate flour mix on three or four parts and add them in three or four batches, using a spatula to fold the mixture together until all is incorporated. Fold in carrots, nuts, and raisins. Drain water from the apricots and pineapples. Dry with a paper towel. Fold in apricots and pineapples.

Step 7: Separate batter into two parts and spread evenly between two greased bowls. Bake until firm for about 25 - 30 minutes or until wooden skewer tester comes clean.

Step 8: Transfer crusts onto cooling racks and peel off the parchment paper if you are using it. Let the cake cool completely.

Make the Frosting:

Step 1: In a bowl of stand mixer fitted with the paddle attachment (you can use a bowl and a hand mixer) combine butter and powdered sugar.

Beat on medium speed for 2 to 3 minutes until it is fully incorporated and becomes fluffy and light in color.

Step 2: Spoon by spoon, add cream cheese and farmers cheese and beat on medium speed for 2 to 3 minutes until it is fully incorporated and becomes light and fluffy.

Add vanilla extract and beat for another 2-3 minutes.

If you decorate your cake using cake decorating piping tips and bags set aside and refrigerate 1/3 of the frosting for about an hour until it becomes firm.

Assemble the Cake:

If you decorate your cake: set aside and refrigerate 1/3 of the frosting for about an hour until it gets firm.

This will be your "cooled frosting". The rest of the frosting will be "room temperature" frosting.

Step 1: If you set aside 1/3 of the frosting for cake decorating, divide the rest of room temperature frosting into three parts. (If not, divide the entire amount of yielded frosting into three parts).

Place a small portion (1-2 tablespoons) of frosting on top of the serving plate.

Step 2: Place the first cake layer on the serving plate and cover top of the crust with 1/4 of the apricot jam. Place 1/3 of the room temperature frosting on top of the jam layer.

Step 3: Place the second layer on top and cover top of the crust with 1/4 of the apricot jam. Place 1/3 of the room temperature frosting on top of the jam layer.

Step 4: Use the remaining 1/3 of room temperature frosting to spread on sides of the cake. Smooth the surface with a spatula.

Use cooled frosting to decorate the cake using piping tips and bags. (Optional).

Decorate the Cake: (optional)

Once you are ready to decorate your cake using piping tips and bags, remove the cooled frosting from the fridge.

Place the cooled frosting into a piping bag and start piping borders and flowers. You can also add food coloring. *(We recommend using natural food coloring instead of artificial colors).*

Store in the refrigerator for up to 5 days or in the fridge for up to one month.

Printed in Great Britain
by Amazon